THE BOY FRC

About the Author

Colin Hayes comes from a naval family. Much of his childhood was spent close to ships and the sea, including two years near Portsmouth where the *Victory* now lies. He now lives and works in East Anglia. The only water nearby is the River Cam; but a favourite weekend haunt is Holkham Bay, only a short distance from Burnham Thorpe and Overy Staithe, where Nelson himself spent so much of his time. Colin Hayes is married to a distant descendant of Nelson, and in their home they have a sword which is *said* to have belonged to Nelson; no one can prove it, but who knows what famous deeds it may once have seen?

THE BOY FROM BURNHAM THORPE

The Story of Lord Nelson

by Colin Hayes

Anglia Young Books

First published in 1989
by Anglia Young Books

Anglia Young Books is an imprint of
Mill Publishing
P.O. Box 120
Bangor
BT19 7BX

Reprinted 2001

Illustrations by Mandy Doyle

Design and production in association with
Book Production Consultants
47 Norfolk Street
Cambridge CB1 2LE

British Library Cataloguing in Publication Data
Hayes, Colin
    The boy from Burnham Thorpe.
    1. Great Britain. Royal Navy. Nelson,
    Horatio Nelson, Viscount –
    Biographies – For children
    I. Title
    359.3'31'0924

    ISBN 1-871173-01-9

Typeset in 11/15 Palatino by Witwell Ltd, Southport
and printed in Great Britain by
W. & G. Baird Ltd.

CONTENTS

AUTHOR'S NOTE

Nelson's life has been so well documented, and he himself wrote so many letters, that we have a very clear idea of what he did and said. In just a few instances in this book I have imagined what Nelson may have said, in order to enliven the narrative; but almost all his remarks have been drawn from reliable sources, and are probably the very words he used.

There are a great number of books about Nelson and his life and times, some of them much better than others. A. T. Mahan's *Life of Nelson*, published in 1897, must still be regarded as one of the very best. Among contemporary works I have made frequent use of *Nelson the Commander* by Geoffrey Bennett and *Horatio Nelson* by Tom Pocock, and I extend my grateful thanks to both authors. Much local and domestic material can be found in *The Nelsons of Burnham Thorpe* by E. E. Matcham, published in 1911, who was a descendant of George Matcham, the husband of Nelson's youngest sister Kitty.

CHAPTER ONE
Poor Horace

Burnham Thorpe is a small village near the north coast of Norfolk. Long ago the salty creeks with their crabs and seaweed and bright seapinks came far inland. Now the sea has retreated behind miles of dunes and marshes, blown by the wild north wind. But when The Reverend Edmund Nelson and Mrs Nelson moved into Burnham Thorpe rectory in 1755 they could still hear the roar of the sea. The rectory was rather modest and cold, but it was somewhere to earn a living and raise a family.

Horatio Nelson was born on September 29th 1758. He was Mrs Nelson's sixth baby. Two had died almost at once, but Maurice, Susanna, and William survived, and then came this rather puny little boy, seven weeks premature. They christened him Horatio because it was a family name; the others thought it was too grand, and he was always known as Horace. The family went on growing, and after

Horace came Anne, Edmund, Suckling and his favourite sister Catherine, known as Kitty: eight of them altogether. But such a big family was quite normal in those days.

Young Horatio loved his home and his family, and country life. In winter the wind blew straight from the North Pole and it was bitterly cold. But in spring and summer the garden, protected by its old brick wall, was a lovely place: full of birdsnests and bumblebees, lavender, and all kinds of fruit – apples, pears, quinces and mulberries. Horatio and his older brother William went to school, and Horatio soon showed that even though he was small he was brave, climbing trees and going birdsnesting where other children were too afraid to go, and able to beat his older brothers in a fight.

In summer there were fairs to go to, and in autumn the harvest celebrations. Sundays were a trial for the small boy, especially as he was the rector's son. The whole village trooped to church in procession, the children dressed in red cloaks, and they sat through long sermons given by Horatio's father. But the Nelsons were happy. And at Burnham Overy and Wells the ships, and sailors' tales, were part of their lives.

When Horatio was nine years old a terrible disaster

struck the family. On Boxing Day Horatio's mother died. She was only forty-two, the last of her eleven babies still only a few months old, but she was worn out. Another blow followed; only a few days later her mother, Horatio's grandmother, died too. There were no aunts or sisters who could come and look after the family so the children were left with only their father, a patient and caring man, but suddenly with all the worries of the world on his shoulders.

The next few years were hard for the Nelson children. Their father never married again, and money was always a problem for he earned only eighty pounds a year when he came to Burnham Thorpe. The biggest worry was how to get the children started in life and off his hands. Soon after their mother's death William and Horatio were sent to the Grammar School at Norwich, and then to a school called Pastons in North Walsham. School life was harsh, and some of the punishments terribly severe. Beatings were frequent, especially for making mistakes in Latin. But Horatio accepted pain like everyone else; it was part of life.

One year, after Christmas, the Reverend Nelson went off to Bath for a rest, leaving the children to themselves. Horatio was restless for adventure, and that was when he had the idea that changed his life.

The boys were reading the Norfolk Chronicle. 'Look at this,' said Horatio, 'it says that we shall soon be at war with Spain. Do you know what that means?' William didn't, as he was not as clever as his younger brother. 'It means,' said Horatio, 'that our Uncle Maurice will be getting ready for action. He is captain of the *Raisonnable*, a man-of-war with 64 guns, and *I* want to go with him. And I want *you* to write to father and get him to arrange it. Please.'

There was a secret to getting on in those days, and Horatio knew as well as anyone what it was. It was called "interest", which meant knowing somebody in a powerful position who could fix things for you. Captain Maurice Suckling was a fine man and a gallant sailor, and the brother of Horatio's mother. Surely he could fix it? But would their father agree?

So the letter went off, and Horatio waited and waited. His father did agree, for he had already resolved that the children should be "brought forward" if possible, which meant sending them out early to earn their living. Horatio was really too young to be a midshipman in the navy, but many people broke the rules in those days. At last came the reply. It was very gruff. 'What has poor Horace done,' wrote Captain Suckling, 'who is so weak, that he above all the rest should be sent to rough it out at sea? But let him come, and the first time we go into action a cannon-ball may blow off his head, and provide for him at once.'

The truth sank in. 'I'm going, I'm going,' cried Horatio. 'I shall have a uniform, and gold buttons. I shall sail the seven seas, and fight for king and country, and be famous!' Things did not move quite so fast, and Horatio had to go back to school for two more months while the *Raisonnable* was made ready for sea. Then at last his instructions arrived. The great day came. He bade his brothers and sisters farewell; travelled with his father to London; then took the stagecoach alone for the slow, bumpy ride to Chatham docks and a life in His Majesty's Navy.

Mr Midshipman Nelson was just twelve years old.

CHAPTER TWO
The Man in the Making

The *Raisonnable* was lying out in the middle of the Medway, and at first Nelson could find no way of getting to her. Then a friendly officer took pity on this lonely little boy and found a ferry for him. But when Nelson stepped on board Captain Suckling was not there, and no one knew who Nelson was. What a strange world he now entered, as he heaved his seachest, containing his few precious belongings, down ladder after ladder to the very depths of the ship, into a dim and twilit world. At last he stood in a gloomy recess with low wooden beams overhead and just the flickering of a tallow lamp. As Nelson's eyes grew used to the semi-darkness he saw his shipmates. Some were boys like himself, and luckily one of them was the son of the customs officer at Wells, so Nelson had a friend from home. But others looked huge and strong, almost old enough to be his father. He felt even smaller than ever.

Life in a man-of-war was a far cry from the peaceful fields of Burnham Thorpe. It was crowded, noisy, dark, and a place where you had to have your wits about you day and night. Older men swore and boasted and drank. The younger ones did as they were told, and tried to do their studies: mathematics, the stars, navigation, all the skills of how to handle a ship, and the art of warfare. They slept in hammocks slung from the ceiling and some had a parrot or even a pet monkey to keep them company. 'Obey orders, learn your duties, and no harm can come to you. That will do,' said the captain to each new boy, and Nelson spent his first three days loading the ship's stores and guns.

The boys did not live the separate lives of officers at this stage, and the seamen with whom they worked were terribly rough. Many of them had been seized by the dreaded Press Gang who rounded men up against their will, and some hated the navy with its savage floggings and life of endless discomfort. The best they could hope for was some prize-money from a battle, and then to be set free.

War did not break out after all, so Nelson did not spend long on the *Raisonnable*. His Uncle Maurice arranged instead for him to go to sea on a merchant ship, the *Mary Ann*. Nelson sailed with her to the West Indies, to Jamaica and Tobago. He loved being at sea, despite being seasick. The ship heeled and creaked her way across the Atlantic; the wind sang in the rigging; sails billowed overhead like clouds; and then at last came the sight of land – tropical islands in the sun. The merchant seamen were a gentler lot than the sailors of the navy, and Nelson got on easily with them. He learned the skills of seamanship from them, and earned their respect. His "touch" with ordinary people was very special, and years later it was the devotion of his fellow-men which helped him to win his great victories.

He was away for a whole year. When he returned Uncle Maurice took him back into a man-of-war in the Thames, and gave him the command of one of the ship's boats, so that Nelson was able to learn the skills of navigating among the sandbanks of the estuary. Then he heard that there was going to be an expedition to the North Pole. Here was another chance for an adventure! He knew that boys were not really allowed, but that did not put him off. He wrote in his diary: 'Nothing could prevent my using every interest to go with Captain Lutwidge in the *Carcass*; and, as I fancied I was to fill a man's place, I begged I might be his coxwain.' Nelson got his way, and in June 1773 set off for the Arctic.

There was another daring boy on the expedition. One foggy night the two of them set out across the ice to try and catch a polar bear, Nelson leading the way. They soon found one; Nelson aimed and fired, but his rusty old musket did not go off. Nelson ignored a signal from the *Carcass* to return. The bear started to attack; Nelson tried to hit it with his musket. A gap opened up in the ice, and that probably saved his life. Then the *Carcass* fired a gun to frighten the bear away. Captain Lutwidge was very stern with Nelson. 'That was conduct unworthy of my crew,' he said. 'Why did you do it?' And young Nelson, trying to think of an honourable excuse, replied: 'Sir, I wished to kill the bear that I might carry its skin to my father.'

For three years he went on more voyages far and wide, and while in the East Indies disaster almost struck again. He fell seriously ill with malaria, the sickening fever that is carried by mosquitos. Only a slim boy at the best of times, he became almost like a skeleton and was close to death. Was his life to end, so soon? Then his spirits rallied. He saw a vision and felt the call of his King and Country. 'Well then,' he cried, 'I will be a hero! And trusting in Providence, I will brave every danger.' Nelson recovered.

Soon he was at sea again. A year later he passed the examination to become a lieutenant, and joined the frigate *Lowestoffe* under Captain Locker, who became his lifelong friend. They sailed to the West Indies once more, to protect England's trade from American ships and also from the French and Spanish. Now he left boyhood behind. Captain Locker gave him a schooner of his own to command, the *Little Lucy*, and told him: 'Lay a Frenchman close, and you will beat him!' so Nelson cruised among the islands, searching for the enemy.

One day, when a violent gale was blowing, the *Lowestoffe* came across an American ship and captured her. The captain needed an officer to board her. Both ships were heaving and tossing in the waves. It was very dangerous and the first lieutenant tried and failed. But when another man came forward Nelson stopped him. 'It is my turn now,' he said, 'and if I come back it is yours.' He succeeded; he had boarded a prize, the dream of every sailor!

Nelson changed ships several times more and rose quickly in rank. Other officers left, or became ill in the sickly climate, and that helped his chances. Then Uncle Maurice Suckling died. Nelson was sad, for his gruff old uncle had done much to help him. But the admiral in the West Indies had already seen that Nelson was a natural leader: brave, quick-witted, and liked by his men. On 11 June 1779, when he was not yet twenty-one, Nelson was made a captain, one of the youngest captains ever. The boy from a Norfolk village was on the brink of his great career.

CHAPTER THREE
In Search of Love and Honour

Captain Nelson took command of the 20-gun frigate *Hinchinbroke* and early in 1780 set sail once more across the Atlantic, his small ship beating through the winter gales to Nicaragua. He had five hundred soldiers with him, because England wanted to find a way across the narrow strip of land between North America and South America and then conquer the Spanish possessions in the Pacific. Here was a chance for action! Even though he was a sailor, Nelson was soon in the thick of things, leading the soldiers up jungle rivers, and shooting at every glimpse of the Spanish enemy. He was joined by Captain Cuthbert Collingwood, who was to become another lifelong friend.

The expedition turned into a disaster. Nelson and all his men were gaunt with dysentery and fever. "Yellow Jack" (which we now call yellow fever) killed all but fifty of the *Hinchinbroke's* crew, and poor Collingwood lost one hundred and eighty of his two hundred men. Nelson was desperately ill, and by the end of the year he had been shipped back to England, barely able to move and close to death.

By now he had been away three whole years. He was taken to his family who were then at Bath for the winter because it was so cold at Burnham Thorpe. He was in great pain, and told a friend: 'I was obliged to be carried to and from bed with the most excruciating tortures.' One arm and thigh were almost paralysed. But he slowly recovered, and was able to enjoy the company of his family whom he had seen so little: brothers Maurice (now a clerk in the Navy Office) and William (a parson), and Susanna and Kitty. He even had a little prize money, a reward for the ships that had been captured, and like most young men he spent the lot!

By the autumn he was back at sea again and more voyages followed, to the Baltic, and then to Newfoundland, but again he fell ill. This time it was scurvy, a disease caused by lack of fresh fruit and vegetables, and Nelson landed in Quebec to recover. There were lots of new people to meet in Quebec, and almost at once he fell in love. Mary Simpson was sixteen, the daughter of the colonel of the garrison. Nelson got on well with her father, and visited her many times. Suddenly his whole world turned upside down. Was a life in the navy really what he wanted? The cold and damp, the discipline and dreadful food, the danger and disease: was it all worth it? He was only twenty-three, but he had been at sea ten years already. Wouldn't life be better in Canada, in love with Mary Simpson? He began to dream of marriage, happiness, and a peaceful home of his own.

Orders came to sail at last, but Nelson walked back into the town instead. Luckily he was spotted by one of his friends, a clever Scottish merchant called Alexander Davison, who asked what he was doing. Nelson replied that he could not leave; he had to 'lay himself and his fortunes at Mary's feet'. Davison was horrified. 'Your utter ruin will inevitably follow,' he said. 'Then let it follow,' Nelson retorted, 'for I am resolved to do it.' 'And I also,' replied Davison, 'positively declare that you shall not.' But somehow Davison made his friend see sense and in the morning Nelson rejoined his ship, heavy of heart. He had avoided a court-martial by the skin of his teeth.

How would the young Captain Nelson have looked to Mary Simpson? He was five feet four inches tall, slightly built but well proportioned. His uniform was handsome: white breeches and waistcoat, a dark tailcoat and three-cornered hat, both edged with thick gold braid, and a sword. His eyes were rather prominent, and his hair often in a mess. But it was his charm which struck people. Prince William, the son of King George III, was one of his friends, and he called him 'the merest boy of a captain I ever beheld ... but there was something irresistibly pleasing in his address and conversation.' When people met Nelson they fell under his spell.

Nelson sailed back to the West Indies again. He so badly wanted success, but before he had a chance peace was declared, and he was out of a job and on half pay. When would he get another chance? He was soon bored and restless, but then he had another of his ideas. England was bound to be at war again, so he would go to France and learn French. That would help him to deal with French captains when he captured them!

He went to St Omer and it wasn't long before he fell in love again, this time to the daughter of an English clergyman. 'She is the most accomplished woman my eyes ever beheld,' he said. He asked his uncle, William Suckling, for money so he could marry her. 'I pray you may never know the pangs which at this instant tear my heart,' he begged. But it seemed that the lady did not wish to accept him, and it came to nothing.

After this disappointment, Nelson received some more bad news: his sister Anne had died. She was only about twenty-two, and had caught a chill after a dance. Nelson was shocked and sad.

He came home when he heard there was to be a general election for Nelson had yet another new idea. He thought he would stand for Parliament, but his enthusiasm for that didn't last long! However, finally Nelson got some good news: even though it was still peacetime the navy gave him a ship to command again, the 28-gun frigate *Boreas*.

Nelson sailed back to the West Indies once more, for another three long years. Again he had hopes of honour and glory, but it was difficult and tedious work in the sticky climate, trying to control traders and seeing that they did not make money dishonestly. He was fed up with the senior officers too. 'The Admiral and all about him are great ninnies,' he remarked. He disobeyed the Admiral and was nearly in serious trouble. Both he and his friend Captain Collingwood became fond of a married lady, and Nelson wrote: 'Were it not for Mrs Moutray who is very, very good to me, I should almost hang myself in this infernal hole.' Then she too went back to England.

But it was in the West Indies that Nelson at last met the lady he was to marry. She was a young widow called Frances Nisbet, with a little boy called Josiah.

Uncle William promised to help out with money, and soon Nelson and Fanny, as he called her, were engaged. Their engagement lasted eighteen months, and Nelson sent Fanny many letters. 'Absent from you I feel no pleasure,' he wrote, 'it is you, my dearest Fanny, who are everything to me. Without you I care not for this world.'

They were married in 1787, when Nelson was twenty-eight, and he wrote once more to his old friend Captain Locker: 'Until I married her, I never knew happiness. I am certain she will make me a happy man for the rest of my days.' Sadly, Nelson was wrong.

CHAPTER FOUR
Becalmed

Nelson and his new bride sailed home. He was happy at last. Winter was coming on, and as neither of them was very well they went once again for a holiday to the milder climate of Bath. The *Boreas* was paid off, and again Nelson was on half pay. He only earned eight shillings a day, but they weren't too worried. Fanny's uncle and Uncle William both gave them a bit more, and no doubt Nelson would soon have another ship. But the months went by, and no news came. Nelson often went to London to visit the Admiralty and to ask for a new command. He tried using all his influence, but it was no good.

'Fanny, my dearest,' he sighed, 'someone must be against me. I have done my best for King and Country. I have saved my country thousands of pounds and made nothing for myself, but much good it has done me. I have not even been thanked for it.'

Then, pacing across the room, he exclaimed: 'Fanny, I'm going to London to resign.'

Fanny may have been secretly delighted to hear this. The sad truth is that she was completely different from her brilliant, energetic, and impulsive husband. She was a slight, nervous, and bird-like woman. After growing up in the West Indies she hated the English climate, and spent days in bed with endless colds. She worried about Nelson whenever he was at sea, and often complained.

Nelson did not resign, but five whole years passed without a ship. At first Fanny and Horatio lived in the rectory with The Reverend Nelson, and he was delighted to have them. He accepted Fanny like another daughter, and Horatio was his favourite son. Young Josiah, Fanny's son, was well looked after too, and together they all helped to keep the place warm, especially in winter. After three years the old man felt they would like the house to themselves so he moved out to a cottage in Burnham Ulph, close to the church. When lunch was ready on a Sunday his housekeeper used to come to the church door, and signal that it was time for the sermon to stop!

But how did Nelson keep himself busy? He did his best to live like a country gentleman. He and Fanny went visiting, to Susanna and her family at

Hilborough, and often to Kitty and her husband at Barton Hall on the Norfolk Broads, where Nelson was embarrassed when his horse bit Kitty's groom in the back! Once or twice they visited the Walpoles, who were relations of Nelson's mother, and Thomas Coke at Holkham Hall. Nelson cultivated his garden, read books, bought a pony at Fakenham market, and hunted hares with dogs. Occasionally he went partridge-shooting, terrifying his friends because he carried his gun at full cock and was liable to loose off without aiming. But his thoughts were elsewhere. On Saturdays he would collect the Norfolk Chronicle and sit by the creek at Overy Staithe, listening to the sound of the far-off sea, and searching for news of war. He even dug a pond in his garden in the shape of a man-of-war. He longed for a child of his own too, but he and Fanny never had any children.

Nelson had a strong sense of fairness, and he became very anxious about the plight of the farm workers in Norfolk. He had known many of them since boyhood, and he hated the way they were treated by the rich landowners. He wrote to his friend Prince William, begging him to do something about them. 'They are more loyal than many of their superiors,' Nelson protested, 'but hunger is a sharp thorn, and they are not only in need of enough food, but of clothes and fuel.' He was right. A labourer earned nine shillings a week. After paying for rent, clothes, candles and coal, he had just fourteen pounds a year to feed his family.

In the village of Burnham Thorpe this was how life went on, but even there, there was already a sense of restlessness. Across the sea in France a storm was gathering that was to change the world. The forces of the French Revolution stormed the Bastille, beheaded the king, and threatened to invade every country in Europe. Suddenly the English awoke. They must fight for their very lives, and now the navy was needed.

Nelson wrote to Fanny from London in great excitement. 'After clouds come sunshine,' he said. (He even wrote it in Latin!) 'Lord Chatham yesterday made many apologies for not having given me a ship before this time, but if I chose to take a 64-gun ship to begin with, I would as soon as possible have a 74.'

Nelson gave a farewell dinner for all his friends at the Plough Inn at Burnham Thorpe (now called the Lord Nelson) but Fanny was miserable. She said she could not possibly stay at Burnham on her own, and went off to live in lodgings at Swaffham. In February 1793, at the age of thirty-five, Nelson once more took the coach to Chatham to command his first big warship, a ship-of-the-line, the *Agamemnon*.

The long wait was over. England was in danger, and
one of her greatest leaders was about to emerge.

CHAPTER FIVE
The Wounded Hero

Nelson's first task was to man the *Agamemnon* and get her ready for sea. He did not like using the terrible Press Gang because it produced violent and bitter men who could not be trusted. He preferred volunteers who would be loyal to him, but it was never easy to find enough. So Nelson sent out a lieutenant and four midshipmen: 'to get men at every seaport in Norfolk, and to send them to Lynn and Yarmouth.' He was still short of a hundred men, but he always said that one Englishman was as good as three Frenchmen! Nelson also had exciting news for young Josiah, who was now thirteen, and for the sons of three other Norfolk parsons: he was taking them with him, and he told them: 'You must hate a Frenchman as you hate the devil!'

The *Agamemnon* sailed to the Mediterranean, and soon she was in action. After the first fierce skirmish under his command Nelson wrote in his journal:

'When I lay me down to sleep I recommend myself to the care of Almighty God; when I awake I give myself up to His direction.' He said prayers before and after all his battles for he was certain that his life was in God's hands. Whatever happened to him, it would be God's will. His father had taught him this, and he believed it to the very end.

Within a year he suffered his first serious wound, while besieging the French in the island of Corsica. Nelson was keen to fight on land because he believed his men were better than soldiers. 'My seamen are almost invincible,' he said. 'They really mind shot no more than peas.' Nelson himself was always in the front, quite fearless, and this was his undoing, both now and later at Trafalgar. A cannonball crashed into the ground beside him, missing his head by inches. Stinging sand flew into his face and eyes. 'I got a little hurt this morning,' he wrote to his Admiral. But the truth was that his right eye, even though it appeared normal, was so damaged that he could only tell light from dark with it.

For two more years Nelson tracked back and forth across the Mediterranean, trying to find the French fleet and bring them to battle. He had more skirmishes, and captured two ships-of-the-line. But the English admirals, unlike Nelson, too often seemed to be timid. They were afraid to take risks. Whenever a good opportunity arose, they pulled back. Nelson was certain he could win a complete victory, if only he had the chance. 'Sure I am,' he wrote after one fight, 'that had I commanded our fleet, either the whole French fleet would have graced my triumph, or I should have been in a confounded scrape.' He was weary and frustrated, and felt like giving up.

Then his luck changed. The great Admiral Sir John Jervis arrived to take command of the fleet. Jervis and Nelson immediately got on well; Jervis saw how brilliant Nelson could be, and that he needed encouragement. 'You must have a larger ship,' he said, 'for we cannot spare you,' and he promoted Nelson to Commodore. Then Nelson bade farewell to his beloved *Agamemnon;* she was battered and worn out, and he took over the 74-gun *Captain.*

Jervis was right. The danger to England was growing month by month. Now a new and dreaded name came on the scene: Bonaparte! Aged only twenty-seven, the young Napoleon Bonaparte took command of the French army in Europe, determined to conquer the world. The Spanish were so alarmed that they decided to join the French. Now the English navy were fighting the French and the Spanish, two enemies at once.

Early in February 1797 Nelson learnt that the

Spanish fleet had sailed past Gibralter into the Atlantic, and he set off in pursuit. One foggy morning the mist lifted for an instant: 'Sail ahoy!' came the cry from the topmast, and there, like a forest above the grey sea, were the masts and spars of the mighty fleet. It was only a glimpse, and the Spanish did not see Nelson. Quickly he got word to Jervis, and on the morning of Valentine's Day the English fleet caught up with them, not far from a headland called Cape St Vincent.

Those men and boys from the villages of Norfolk must have gazed on a sight to turn their blood cold: twenty-seven Spanish ships-of-the-line and ten frigates; almost twice as many as the English. Seven Spanish ships with more than a hundred guns each, and towering above them the biggest warship in the world, the *Santissima Trinidad*, with four decks of guns, like a castle astride the waves.

The two fleets started to form up in two long lines, opposite each other, which is how sea-battles were usually fought. Suddenly Nelson saw that the enemy might again slip away. Against all instructions he turned the *Captain* round and went straight for two of the Spanish. Collingwood, in another ship, did the same. A furious battle followed. Down came the *Captain's* mast, and down too fell many of her men. The two Spanish ships got locked together. The

Captain drifted onto them, and at once Nelson called 'Prepare to board!' Then with a shout of 'Westminster Abbey, or glorious victory!' he led the fighting as his men crashed through the upper windows of the *San Nicolas*. After a fierce fight the Spanish captain was on bended knee before him, offering him his sword in surrender, while the admiral died of his wounds below. Nelson captured both ships together, the first time it had ever been done, and later presented the Spanish admiral's sword to the city of Norwich. As Jervis sailed past them in the *Victory* he called 'Three cheers for Commodore Nelson!' The Spanish fleet was in disarray. Victory, victory at last!

Later that day Nelson climbed painfully aboard the *Victory*. He was bruised and dirty, and part of his hat was missing. Admiral Jervis embraced him, and thanked him again and again. A jealous captain pointed out that Nelson had disobeyed all the rules by turning his ship out of the line. 'It certainly was so,' said wise old Jervis, 'and if ever you commit such a breach, I will forgive you also.'

Rewards came thick and fast for the victorious English. Nelson became Rear Admiral Sir Horatio Nelson, with a pension of a thousand pounds a year for life. But Fanny's reaction, when she heard his news, was as nervous as ever. 'Thank God you are well,' she wrote. 'My anxiety was far beyond my powers of expression. You have done desperate actions enough. Now may I beg that you never board again.'

Fanny's words were in vain. Nelson remained at sea, looking for yet more chances of success. First he got involved in a hand to hand sword fight, trying to capture a Spanish gunboat, and barely escaped with his life. Then he led an attack on a Spanish island to seize a treasure-ship. It was a disaster. As Nelson stepped ashore and drew his sword a bullet shattered his right arm. He fell unconscious, blood pouring out. Josiah, now a lieutenant, rushed to staunch the flow. When they got back to the ship Nelson insisted on walking aboard despite the terrible pain, and saluted with his left hand. The ship's doctor sawed off his arm at once, without anaesthetic, and stitched him up. 'Ten minutes longer,' said Nelson, 'and I would have been no more.'

Now he had to go home. He was in pain, and annoyed with himself, and his thoughts turned once more to the peace and quiet of his Norfolk garden. Sir Horatio Nelson sailed into Portsmouth on September 1st 1797. Crowds packed the quayside and thronged the streets, cheering, weeping with joy, and throwing their hats in the air. Nelson had lost an eye and an arm, but England had found a new hero.

CHAPTER SIX
Lord Nelson of The Nile and Burnham Thorpe

Nelson sped to Bath to rejoin Fanny as fast as he could. It was four whole years since he had seen his family. Fanny, his father, and Susanna received him with open arms, and the rest of the family soon turned up to join in the celebrations. Nelson and Fanny, after their long separation, were now as happy as they had ever been. She was able to worry about her wounded husband and dressed the stump of his arm every day, though she did not like doing it much.

'I found my domestic happiness perfect,' Nelson wrote to Jervis (who had now become Lord St Vincent). Soon after this he bought Roundwood, a six-bedroomed house near Ipswich, so that Fanny could live in more style and comfort, although – as we shall see – he never lived there himself. He taught himself to write left-handed, and designed an ingenious fork with a knife along one edge so that he could eat with one hand. On his coat he wore the star of the Order of the Bath, denoting his knighthood, which everyone could see and admire. He was extremely proud of it.

Even so, Nelson was always going to the Admiralty to get news of the war, and could hardly bear to be stuck on dry land. Then one morning he awoke without pain. The stump had healed, and he was fit to go to sea again! That night at dinner Nelson told everyone how happy he was to be with Fanny; the very next day he urged her to move into Roundwood, while he prepared for sea. But even then Fanny made a muddle of his packing. It was the last time they were ever to be happy together.

Nelson set sail in the *Vanguard*, another 74-gun ship, and rejoined Lord St Vincent near Gibraltar. He took with him Tom Allen, a servant from Burnham Thorpe, to help him dress and eat, and to look after him. The admiral's cabin on board a flagship was a very good place to work; it was like a room in a house, with a fine table and chairs, silver cutlery, carpets, and elegant windows. But Nelson was rather crotchety with his one arm, and poor Tom had a hard time keeping his master comfortable. Little could he have guessed that he was to witness one of the greatest sea battles in history.

By now the French had put Bonaparte in command of an "Army of the East", with secret instructions to occupy Egypt, and then to destroy British power in India. Lord St Vincent immediately gave Nelson, who was now in command of a squadron of ships, the job of leading the search for the French. Nelson was in trouble almost at once, for a violent storm blew up and the *Vanguard* lost her masts, but as soon as she was repaired he held a council of war with his captains. Where was the French fleet? Where was Bonaparte heading? To Malta, Italy, Sicily, Egypt, even England; all were possibilities. They guessed Egypt and the chase began!

They sailed across the Mediterranean to Egypt as fast as wind and sail would allow. No French fleet. Well then, Sicily? Back they went, hundreds of miles. Still no French fleet. 'It broke my heart,' said Nelson. But his instinct told him that it *must* be at Egypt, and then he intercepted a ship and was told that the French had indeed been spotted heading that way. They sped back. On August 1st 1798 at 1 p.m. they glimpsed the coast of Aboukir Bay, near the mouth of the River Nile, and once more came the cry from the topmast: 'Sail-oh!' The French were there. The men of the *Vanguard* gave three cheers and Nelson, who had hardly eaten or slept for days, drank what he called "a bumper toast" and sat down to a good lunch. 'Before this time tomorrow,' he said, 'I shall have gained a peerage or Westminster Abbey.'

Midsummer in Egypt. A hot and sleepy afternoon. It would be dark by seven. The French were moored in line ahead, thirteen ships-of-the-line, close to the shore for safety. Both fleets hoisted the signal "Prepare for Battle", but the French admiral did not think the English would start to fight so late in the day. Nelson thought differently. Now for the first time, at the age of nearly forty, he was to reveal his greatness. The genius of a great commander is to take the enemy by surprise, and then to fight to the finish. All his captains, whom he called his "Band of Brothers", knew what they had to do.

Inching their way past the sandbanks, the leading English ships crept between the French line and the shore, which the French had thought was impossible, while the remainder went the other side. As dusk fell the night sky was shattered by the roar of broadsides as Nelson's ships pounded the pride of the French fleet from both sides. More than twenty ships, almost next to each other in the dark, poured their fire into each other. Masts and rigging fell, splinters flew, and there were terrible casualties. Quite early on Nelson was struck on the forehead by a flying piece of iron, tearing the skin down over his eyes. He cried out 'I am killed: remember me to my wife!' and was carried below.

The French fought with great bravery, but they had been caught napping and the front of their line was outnumbered. Then their flagship, the majestic *L'Orient* of 120 guns, caught fire – a terrifying and dreadful sight. Other ships struggled to back away. At 10 o'clock she blew to pieces with a roar that shook the sky fifteen miles away. Down with her to the bottom went almost all her men. Down too sank the treasure which Napoleon had seized from the Knights of Malta on his way to Egypt. For several minutes there was the shock of silence, as firing ceased and sailors from both sides tried to pick up the survivors. Then battle resumed. Nelson came back on deck, his head bandaged, and took command again. By morning all but two of the French ships-of-the-line had been captured or burnt. The English were battered and exhausted, but had lost none. Bonaparte was marooned in Egypt, his fleet destroyed. It was the most glorious naval victory in living memory.

It was two months before the news found its way to England, first by ship across the Mediterranean and then overland through Europe. Imagine the scenes in London! The First Lord of the Admiralty fainted in Whitehall when he heard the news. Guns fired from the Tower of London and in the parks. There was wild excitement in the streets. The printing machines of the London Gazette clattered into life to rush off an "Extraordinary Edition", carried by thundering mailcoaches across the length and breadth of the land.

Imagine too the scene in the town of Beccles, where The Reverend Nelson had been a curate and he and Nelson's mother had been married. It was a normal market day, the harvest safely in, nothing out of the ordinary. Then the mailcoach swept in, the Gazette passed swiftly from hand to hand, and in no time the bells were ringing out to villages far and near. Bonfires blazed, bands played, and people danced in the streets to a new tune called "Nelson's Fancy". A bellringer wrote in his diary: '1798 October. Great news from Horatio Nelson, who took nine ships of the line. Wringing.' He may have been a keen bellringer, but he was a bad speller! In Burnham Thorpe they ran to congratulate The Reverend Nelson, and to Fanny they said: 'Mark you, they'll make him a Lord, and you will be Lady Nelson.' At Ipswich they held a grand ball, with Fanny as the guest of honour.

Nelson was made Baron of the Nile and Burnham Thorpe. Parliament thanked him and awarded him a pension of £2000 a year for life – a lot of money in those days, and the East India Company sent him the huge gift of £10,000 for saving their business. Nelson gave £500 to each of his brothers and sisters, and paid for his old father to have a proper carriage and a servant. His friend Davison made gold, silver and bronze medals for everyone who had been at the battle and even Josiah, who was not a good officer, was made a captain.

But Nelson did not come home. He went to Naples in Italy, and there, in his hour of glory, he began a love-affair which tarnished his reputation for ever.

CHAPTER SEVEN
Emma

Nelson sailed to Naples to ask King Ferdinand (who was king of Sicily and part of Italy) to help him against the French. His head was still badly wounded, and he thought much of home and Fanny. 'May God bless you, my dearest Fanny,' he wrote, 'and give us in due time a happy meeting.' He called her: 'My dearest wife, my friend, my everything which is most dear to me in this world.' But his fateful stay in Naples and Sicily changed their lives.

The English ambassador to the court of Naples was an elderly man called Sir William Hamilton. His wife, who was then thirty-three and half his age, was called Emma. She was a beautiful woman, quite large, with dark eyes and tumbling, dark curls. She had started life as a servant, but she could sing and act, and had lived with other men before old Sir William married her. Emma had met Nelson briefly five years before, and she had never forgotten him. She had been kind to Josiah too, which Nelson remembered. Even before he reached Naples she had dressed herself in the colours of the navy, and was riding round with a scarf on her head bearing the words "Nelson and Victory". As soon as she and Sir William came on board Nelson's flagship the *Vanguard* Emma cried out; 'Oh God, is it possible?' and threw herself upon Nelson.

Nelson was at first rather embarrassed, but it did not take Emma long to find her way into his heart. She told him how brave and brilliant he was, which Fanny had never done, and she also helped him at the royal court. Nelson fell completely under her spell. Soon he was writing: 'Lady Hamilton is an Angel', and 'Her head and heart surpass her beauty'. Worst of all, he even wrote to Fanny: 'Lady Hamilton is one of the very best women in this world.'

Sir William and Nelson became close friends too, so when the three of them moved to Sicily, Nelson moved in with the Hamiltons. The gossip flowed thick and fast: stories of expensive parties (paid for by Nelson) and playing cards all night, and Emma losing all Nelson's money. 'She leads him about,' said one of Nelson's friends, 'Like a keeper with a bear.'

Nelson stayed two years in the Mediterranean,

involved in politics, and becoming more and more in love with Emma. King Ferdinand made him Duke of Bronte in Sicily, and awarded him yet more decorations. It was then that Nelson became pompous and vain. He disobeyed his superiors, covered himself with medals, and deceived Fanny, but he was not really happy. His health was breaking down, and he asked to come home, even saying that he would not serve again in the navy. The Admiralty already knew that he was behaving badly, so they let him come. Finally the Hamiltons and Nelson set off for England together, on a kind of triumphal tour through Europe. And by this time Emma was expecting Nelson's baby.

They landed at Yarmouth on November 6th, 1800, more than two years after The Battle of the Nile. Ordinary folk in England were not concerned about the gossip. On the contrary, they now had in Nelson the kind of hero they needed in their fight against Bonaparte, and the kind of person they could really admire. For Nelson was not a rich aristocrat from another class; he was one of them, with all their own human weaknesses. So the people of Yarmouth gave their hero a tumultuous welcome; bands played, speeches were made, and they hauled his carriage through the streets. The landlady of The Wrestlers Inn asked if she could name it The Nelson Arms;

'That would be absurd,' Nelson joked: 'I have only got one!'

Then Nelson had to face Fanny. She and his father came to meet him in a hotel in London. He seemed to hope that they could all get along together and he even took Fanny to dinner with the Hamiltons, telling her what a wonderful person Emma was. Poor Fanny; it was an impossible situation for her. She and Nelson began to quarrel, and finally the explosion came. Fanny burst out: 'I am sick of hearing of dear Lady Hamilton. I am resolved that you shall give up her or me.' 'Take care, Fanny, what you say,' Nelson replied. 'I love you sincerely, but I cannot forget my obligations to Lady Hamilton.' It was too much. They parted in anger, never to see each other again. Two weeks later Emma had a baby girl, and named her Horatia.

Nelson was overjoyed at the birth of his daughter, but he had no chance to see her. He had already become a Vice Admiral and was appointed to join the Home Fleet, for he was needed again. This time it was Russia and Denmark who seemed ready to join with the French, and England had to stop them. The Baltic Sea was a very important area for England's trade, especially timber. Many old houses in East Anglia have wooden beams in their ceilings from the Baltic.

On April 2nd, 1801, the English fleet fought the Danish at the Battle of Copenhagen. The English had a rather cautious Commander-in-Chief called Sir Hyde Parker. Once again it was Nelson who pressed forward and brought the Danes to battle. It was a desperately hard fight, much closer than at the Nile and the Danes fought with great determination. Parker became very worried, and hoisted a signal telling Nelson's ships to withdraw. Once again Nelson refused to obey. 'Leave off action? he exclaimed. 'Now damn me if I do!' Turning to his captain he said: 'You know I have only one eye. I have a right to blindness sometimes.' Then he put his telescope to his blind eye and said: 'I really do not see the signal!'

They battled on, and once again it was Nelson who won another great victory, for which he was made a Viscount. But he was uncomfortable in the bitter cold weather of the Baltic. He almost caught pneumonia after spending a night in an open boat, and again asked to come home. 'The keen air of the North kills me,' he wrote. And to Emma he said: 'I am fixed to live a country life, and to have many (I hope) years of comfort, which, God knows, I never yet had ...'

Nelson returned to England, landing once more at Yarmouth. He had one more action that year. It was thought the French army was preparing to invade

England from across the Channel so Nelson tried to raid Boulogne, but this time the French were well prepared and he failed. After that he bought a beautiful house at Merton, near Wimbledon, and settled down again with the Hamiltons. Roundwood, the house he had bought for Fanny, was sold.

Fanny tried hard to keep in touch with Nelson and make amends, but Nelson did not want to see her again. He gave her enough money to be able to live comfortably, and asked her to leave him alone. At the end of the year she wrote him one last letter. 'Do, my dear husband, let us live together,' Fanny begged. 'I have but one wish in the world, to please you.' The letter was returned with a note written by Davison: 'Opened by mistake by Lord Nelson, but not read.' It was a cruel way to say goodbye.

CHAPTER EIGHT
His Work Is Done

Late in 1801 a truce was agreed with France. Nelson was free to go on leave at last, and then to remain at home on half-pay. 'Thank God it is peace!' he said. We remember Nelson for his battles, but we must also remember that he only fought them to defend his country. In a speech to Parliament he said: 'I have seen much of the miseries of war. I am therefore in my inmost soul a man of peace.' But despite the truce, he still did not trust Bonaparte.

Nelson and Emma settled at Merton for nearly two years. Little Horatia lived with a foster-mother in London, so that Sir William would not be embarrassed, and they made secret visits to see her. These were happy times for them both, marred only by the deaths first of Nelson's father, and then of Sir William. Sadly too, the old parsonage at Burnham Thorpe was pulled down.

But the peace of their country life was shattered as

Bonaparte became the Emperor Napoleon, and threatened Europe once more. England declared war again and by now, five years after the Battle of the Nile, Napoleon had rebuilt his fleet. People were so afraid of an invasion that in Norfolk bonfires were forbidden, in case they caused a false alarm. 'Whenever it is necessary, I am your admiral,' Nelson wrote to the Prime Minister. He was made Commander-in-Chief of the Mediterranean Fleet, with the *Victory* as his flagship.

Nelson was now close to the pinnacle of his great career. At last he was in command. He had won the honour and glory which he had sought as a young man. He did not need to be vain and pompous any more, and was calm and determined. He had one job to do: to bring the French fleet to battle and destroy it, so that England could not be invaded.

For two years Nelson stayed at sea, often in terrible weather, and never setting foot on land. All this time he had to keep his ships seaworthy and their men healthy and in good heart. He made sure that they had plenty of onions, good mutton, beef, fresh water, and rum. Even so, Captain Hardy had many of the *Victory's* men flogged to keep them in order. When the French ships at last put to sea they headed for the West Indies. Nelson chased them right across the Atlantic, and all the way back again, without finding them. It was heartbreaking work, and he would not even let Emma join him after her next baby died. 'Your Nelson is called upon to defend his country,' he told her sternly.

In August 1805 Nelson returned to Merton for a rest, very tired and downcast. There he met Emma again and Horatia, now a little girl of four. He was very proud of his daughter, and gave her a silver cup with her name on it. Many of the family came to see them. If only he could rest from his labours now! But Napoleon was already just across the Channel at Boulogne, and the French and Spanish fleets had been seen at last near Spain. Nelson had to go. 'I drove from dear, dear Merton,' he wrote, 'where I left all which I hold dear in this world, to go to serve my King and Country.' The crowds at Portsmouth waved and cheered and many wept. Nelson waved his hat in reply, never to return.

The fleet which Nelson joined contained several captains who had not served with him before, but in no time he had inspired them with his confidence and told them his plan of attack. His second-in-command was his old and trusted friend Admiral Collingwood, and Captain Hardy of the *Victory* who had been with him in all his great battles was with him again. So his new "Band of Brothers" were all under the spell of the "Nelson touch".

Dawn broke on October 21st 1805. Nelson's fleet of twenty-seven ships was opposite Cape Trafalgar, not far from the straits of Gibraltar, and there, ten miles away, were the thirty-three ships of the enemy! The lightest breeze ruffled a gentle, rolling swell. For several hours the two great fleets converged almost in slow motion. Time for sailors to write their last letters home (Nelson was thoughtful about his men's feelings to the end, and even called a boat back to collect one sailor's letter that had been missed). Time for the ships' bands to strike up with stirring tunes such as Rule Britannia, and Hearts of Oak. Time for Nelson to remark: 'This is the happiest day of my life, and it is a happy day too at Burnham Thorpe; this is the day of the fair.'

Time then for Nelson to go to his cabin, pen his own last letters to Emma and Horatia, and write his will, in which he asked his country to care for them. Time, finally, for him to kneel down and write one last noble prayer: 'May the Great God whom I worship grant to my country and for the benefit of Europe in general a great and glorious victory ...' And he finished: 'To Him I resign myself ... Amen, Amen, Amen.'

By noon the fleets were close enough to engage. As a last encouragement to his men Nelson hoisted the signal: 'England expects that every man will do his duty.' Collingwood muttered: 'I wish Nelson would stop sending signals; we all know what to do!' Then the two columns of English ships, one led by Nelson in the *Victory*, the other by Collingwood in the *Royal Sovereign*, pierced the long line of the French and Spanish fleet, and the sleepy day was rent by the crash of a thousand cannons.

Nelson paced up and down his deck with Hardy as the battle raged around them, the bright stars on his coat clearly visible. Fifty feet above, in the rigging of the French ship alongside him, musketeers poured their fire down on the deck of the Victory. Hardy saw Nelson fall to the deck. 'I trust you are not badly hurt?' he asked anxiously. Nelson gasped 'They have done for me at last. My back-bone is shot through.' This time he was right. The shot from above had caught him in the shoulder, and then passed through his lung and spine, cutting an artery on the way. They carried him below, his face and medals covered with a handkerchief so that his men should not know that their leader had fallen.

The cockpit was hot and filled with wounded and dying men. The ship's doctor gently undressed Nelson and propped him against a bulkhead. Other officers and the chaplain stood around in the half-darkness. They gave him lemonade, fanned him, and tried to ease the waves of pain, while above the guns roared and the air was filled with cries and smoke. 'Oh *Victory, Victory,* how you distract my poor brain,' Nelson sighed, speaking to the ship in his distress. But all the time he was anxious for Hardy, and news of the battle. When Hardy came, Nelson heard at last of the success which he had sought for so long. 'God be praised, I have done my duty,' he said, and he repeated this many times.

From then on his life ebbed quietly away. His thoughts turned often to Emma and Horatia, and to his own home. An hour later Hardy came again, told Nelson how great the triumph was, and clasped his hand. At least fourteen or fifteen of the French and Spanish ships had been captured, he said (in fact it was even more) and not a single English ship had been lost. Even then Nelson replied: 'That is well, but I bargained for twenty,' and gave more orders. But his strength was almost gone. 'Don't throw me overboard; you know what to do,' he said to Hardy, thinking again of his parents' grave at Burnham Thorpe. 'Take care of my dear Lady Hamilton,' he went on, then commanded Hardy to kiss him. (Such gestures were quite normal. Jervis kissed Nelson after the Battle of Cape St Vincent) 'Now I am satisfied,' he sighed again. 'Thank God I have done my duty.' The doctor

heard him whisper 'God and my country' one more time. Then Nelson closed his eyes for ever.

The news took only two weeks to reach England. Again the London Gazette was rushed across the land, and again the bells rang out in Beccles, but now they were mixed with sadness as much as joy. Nelson's last letter to Emma was taken to her. 'Oh miserable, wretched Emma!' she wrote on it in shaky writing; 'Oh glorious and happy Nelson!' Nelson's body was carried home, preserved in spirits, and lay in state at Greenwich. Then the funeral procession, with thunder and lightning bursting overhead, took him to be buried in the crypt of St Pauls, with three of his "Band of Brothers" beside him. Thirty-one admirals and a hundred captains walked behind. All London stopped, and even the thieves and beggars came out from their dark alleys to watch their dead hero pass.

· · · · ·

The Battle of Trafalgar was a turning point in history. Thanks to Nelson, Napoleon was unable to command the seas, and he never invaded England. The Battle of Waterloo, ten years later, finally brought peace between England and Europe, and it lasted for a hundred years.

Nelson's column in Trafalgar Square is a fine monument to such a great man, but it is not really like him. It is stiff and grand, and thronged by traffic and tourists. We should think of him surrounded by his captains and his friends; small, lively, sometimes moody, often affectionate; happiest with the sea-breeze in his face, or in his garden at Burnham Thorpe.

And what of the others? Emma spent all her money, got into debt, drank heavily, and died in Calais. Josiah had already left the navy, and became a rich business-man. Horatia grew up to look just like her father, married a clergyman, and lived to a great age. And Fanny, despite her broken heart, settled in quiet retirement, and treasured the memory of her husband until the day she died.

PLACES TO VISIT

Burnham Thorpe: The Church, where Nelson's parents (but not Nelson himself) are buried; and The Lord Nelson Inn, where there are lots of things to do with him. Burnham Overy Staithe, Wells, Holkham Hall, and Fakenham, are all nearby, and Burnham Market, where The Reverend Nelson retired.

Beccles: The church, where The Reverend Nelson was curate and Nelson's parents were married.

Yarmouth: The Nelson monument and The Wrestlers Inn.

Barton: Barton Hall, where Nelson's favourite sister Kitty lived, and he used to visit.

Norwich: The museum, and Norwich School (which has a statue of Nelson outside it).

London: The Nelson monument in Trafalgar Square; the crypt of St Pauls Cathedral where Nelson is buried; and the National Maritime Museum at Greenwich, where there are many paintings, documents and other relics of the Nelson era.

Portsmouth: HMS *Victory*, preserved as she was at the time of Trafalgar, showing the spot where Nelson fell and the cockpit where he died.

Monmouth: There is a Nelson museum here as well, which contains many of his original letters.